Mystery Shopping Restaurants

GET PAID TO EAT
IN YOUR FAVORITE RESTAURANTS

Cathy Stucker

Special Interests Publishing
SUGAR LAND, TEXAS

Special Interests Publishing
www.sipub.com

Book Layout © BookDesignTemplates.com

Ordering Information:
Quantity sales. Special discounts are available on quantity purchases by corporations, associations, and others. For details, contact the author at cathy@idealady.com.

Mystery Shopping Restaurants/ Cathy Stucker. —1st ed.
ISBN 978-1-888983-52-4

Contents

You notice (hospitality) when it's there, and you particularly notice it when it isn't.

A single significant lapse in this area can be your dominant impression of an entire meal.

John Lanchester

CHAPTER 1

Introduction

Whether or not you are currently mystery shopping, this book will provide you with the information you need to become a successful restaurant mystery shopper. If you are an experienced mystery shopper, you will get advice and tips that will help you step up your game in order to get more and better restaurant assignments. If you have never mystery shopped before, the information in the final chapter will show you how to get started, and with what you learn in the rest of the book, you will be off to a running start in building a successful mystery shopping career.

I have been a mystery shopper since 1995, and I have shopped all kinds of businesses. However, restaurants are my favorites. My husband and I go out to eat at least once a week, so we love to mystery shop restaurants. In my opinion, the only thing better than eating food I don't have to cook is not having to pay for that food, either!

Even though our meals are paid for when we do shops, it is not truly "free" food. That is because there is a catch. I have to make observations and complete a report telling what happened during our visit. That, however, is a trade-off I am more than happy to make. In exchange for a bit of time completing reports, we have eaten meals ranging from fast food hamburgers to deluxe steak dinners.

Keep reading to find out how you can become a mystery shopper and start getting paid to go to some of your favorite restaurants.

An Important Note:

There is nothing that is done exactly the same way by every mystery shopping company for every client. In this book, I am sharing practices that are common and typical in the industry, but there are exceptions to everything.

Always carefully read the guidelines before doing a shop. If anything is not clear, consult with your scheduler to learn what is expected.

CHAPTER 2

What is Mystery Shopping?

Mystery shoppers evaluate customer service, cleanliness and quality at all kinds of businesses. The mystery shopper reports are used by businesses to recognize star performers, determine training needs, monitor whether procedures are being followed, identify missed sales opportunities and even, in some cases, as one factor in determining raises and bonuses.

Secret shopping programs are used in many businesses, including retail stores, restaurants, hotels, banks, apartment complexes, movie theaters, automotive sales and service, spas, salons, and just about everywhere else that does business with the public. Even government agencies may be mystery shopped. In this book, we are going to focus on restaurant mystery shopping, but you do not have to limit yourself to only shopping one type of business. You will have opportunities to do many kinds of mystery shops.

What Do Mystery Shoppers Do?

Mystery shoppers visit businesses and act like normal customers. However, the mystery shopper has been given a list of questions that they are to answer in a report completed after the visit. These questions may address issues such as how long they were in the business before they were greeted, if suggestive selling techniques were used, whether or not they were thanked, if the location was clean and well-maintained, etc.

A mystery shopper should not let anyone know that they are conducting the evaluation. They simply appear to be a customer, doing the things typical customers do, such as asking questions and making a purchase.

Later, the shopper will complete a report form (usually online) to answer the questions they were given prior to the visit.

Although a common perception is that we give our opinions about things such as food quality, service and cleanliness, mystery shoppers actually report facts. As a restaurant mystery shopper you will function more as a reporter than as a food critic.

A food critic offers opinions about their dining experiences. Mystery shoppers do not give our opinions of the food and service, we are reporting facts.

Before going to the restaurant, we are given a report form that will be completed after the visit. Although there may be a few opinion questions on the report, most of the report will contain objective questions, such as:

- Was your reservation time honored? If not, how long did you have to wait?
- How long after you were seated did your server arrive at the table?
- Did the server introduce him/herself?
- Did the server suggest a specific appetizer? If so, what did s/he suggest?
- How much time elapsed between the time you ordered and the time you were served?
    - Beverages
    - Appetizer or salad
    - Dessert
- How long after your appetizer was cleared was your entrée served?
- Did the server perform a satisfaction check within one minute after your food was served?
- Were all items prepared as ordered?
- Were beverages refilled before they were 2/3 empty?
- Was your check correct and were you charged for all items ordered?

Restaurant shops will typically require several timings, sometimes to the second. There will usually be questions about the cleanliness of the facility, including the rest rooms. And there will be other, client-specific questions about what happened while you were there.

Although a mystery shop report will include questions about food quality, that is just one piece of the puzzle.

Mystery shop reports give a picture of the entire customer experience

Types of Restaurants

To be a good restaurant mystery shopper, you should have a general idea of how restaurants are classified. Some restaurant mystery shop reports will ask questions about how a location compares to similar restaurants in the area, or where you would have dined if you had not visited their restaurant. They are looking for who you consider their prime competitors to be in the area. Saying that if you had not gotten a steak at Ruth's Chris you would have grabbed a burger and fries at McDonald's would not be the answer they are looking for.

There are five major types of restaurants. Although the names and definitions vary a bit, based on who is talking about them, most industry sources classify restaurants in the following categories:

Fast Food (or Quick Service)

You may see job postings for QSRs. That stands for Quick Service Restaurants, which are the same as fast food. In fast food, customers typically order at the counter and take their own food to their tables. Some fast food restaurants may not have seating but only offer take away service. Many fast food locations feature drive-through service where customers can order and receive food in their cars.

Food served at fast food restaurants may include hamburgers, chicken, sandwiches, tacos and barbecue. Examples of fast food restaurants include:

- McDonald's
- Wendy's
- Burger King
- Arby's
- KFC

Mystery shops at fast food restaurants may be for dining in the restaurant, getting your food at the drive-through or both. These shops are more likely than others to specify exactly what you must order. For example, you may be told to order a specific sandwich or combo.

Because timings are a critical part of these shops, you may be told not to make any special requests (such as "no pickles") with your order.

Fast Casual

Fast casual is a step up from fast food. Customers at fast casual restaurants typically order at a counter, but there may be some table service. For example, food may be delivered to the table, or staff my offer beverage refills and other service. Food at fast casual restaurants may feature more fresh ingredients than typical fast food fare. Some may offer non-disposable serving dishes and cutlery.

Food served at fast casual restaurants may include ethnic varieties, such as Mexican or Asian, as well as hamburgers, sandwiches, salads and other traditional American fare. A few fast casual restaurants offer beer, wine or a limited liquor selection. Some of the restaurants classified as fast casual include:

- Jason's Deli
- Noodles and Company
- Chipotle
- Panera Bread
- Panda Express

Casual Dining

Casual dining restaurants feature full table service and many offer beer, wine and liquor. Although they may offer some of the same types of food as fast food restaurants (e.g., burgers, etc.) their versions (and prices) are more upscale. Non-disposable serving utensils are used. Most casual dining restaurants do not take reservations, although some allow customers to call ahead or register using an app to hold a spot in line.

There are many, many local, regional, national and international casual dining restaurants, including:

- Outback
- Olive Garden
- P.F. Chang's
- Chili's

- Red Lobster
- The Cheesecake Factory

Fine Dining

Fine dining restaurants are upscale in appearance, menu and service. Staff may be formally dressed, and there may also be a dress code for customers. Steak and seafood are typical menu items. There is typically a full bar with an extensive wine list.

Reservations are often recommended or required, especially for weekend dinners and special occasions, such as Valentine's Day and Mother's Day. Mystery shoppers are usually told not to make a shop visit on a holiday as those days are much busier than normal. Also, the restaurant may have a special or limited menu for the holiday.

Examples of fine dining chains include:
- Ruth's Chris
- The Capital Grille
- Morton's
- McCormick and Schmick

Each of these types of restaurants gets mystery shopped. The nature of these shops will depend on the type of establishment being evaluated.

CHAPTER 4

How Much Do Mystery Shoppers Get Paid?

Pay for mystery shopping is generally by the job, not by the hour. The amount a shopper receives for completing an assignment will vary, based on the time required to complete the shop and report, any required purchases, special skills needed, and other factors.

Secret shopper pay may be a flat fee, a reimbursement for a required purchase, or both a fee and reimbursement. For example, compensation for a restaurant mystery shop is often reimbursement for meals for two people (the shopper and a companion) and it may also include a small fee, such as $5 to $10.

Do not underestimate the value of reimbursements. Although at the low end reimbursements may not amount to much, on some assignments the reimbursement may be well over $100. I have done fine dining shops that included a reimbursement of more than $200.

The total amount a shopper will earn depends on where she lives, the number of shops he is willing and able to do, the type of shop assignments accepted and the quality of the shopper's work. With some experience, many part-time shoppers make $500 – $1000 a month or more, working a schedule of their choosing. If most of those shops are restaurant shops, the majority of that compensation will be reimbursement for meals purchased on shops. However, there are many other types of shops that are fee-based, and not mostly reimbursement.

You can choose the types of shops you will do based on what you enjoy. You may also decide whether you prefer most of your compensation to come in the form of reimbursement or cash fees and choose assignments accordingly.

CHAPTER 5

Choosing Assignments

The compensation for some restaurant mystery shops consists of a fee and reimbursement for the required purchase. Other types of shops, such as those without a required purchase (including banks, apartment complexes and car dealerships), will not include a reimbursement, but may have a higher fee.

Should You Do Reimbursement-Only Shops?

But what about mystery shops where your only compensation is the reimbursement of the required purchase, with no fee? Some shoppers refuse to do reimbursement-only shops, and will only accept assignments that include a fee.

Although most of the shops I do include a fee, there are times when I do reimbursement-only restaurant shops. My husband and I enjoy going out to dinner, so getting our dinner paid for in return for a mystery shop report can be, in some situations, a good deal. Just for the record, we are not talking about fast food here, but nice restaurants involving servers and often alcohol. And definitely dessert.

Ultimately, decisions about which shops you will do are up to you. You decide how much compensation makes a shop worthwhile, and whether or not you are willing to do reimbursement-only shops.

Here are some factors to consider in making your decision.

What is the value of the reimbursement?

I have done shops (with or without a fee) that included reimbursements of $150 or more. When calculated over the time required to do the shop and report, that can be a great hourly rate.

What is the value of the reimbursement to you?

If you do not want or need the purchase for which you are reimbursed, it doesn't matter how much the reimbursement is. A fine dining shop may not be enjoyable if you are on a diet and have to watch what you eat, just as a vision shop is not useful if you don't need a new pair of glasses.

Even if the shop offers a large reimbursement, if it is not valuable to you it is not worthwhile. If the reimbursement is for something you would have purchased even if you weren't doing a mystery shop, then it may be a good deal.

Is the reimbursement adequate to cover the required purchase?

This seems obvious: If you are doing a shop solely for reimbursement, the reimbursement ought to at least cover what you are required to buy. However, there are shops where the required purchase will always be greater than the maximum reimbursement. If you are not certain how much the typical purchase would be, ask your scheduler for more information.

Can you afford to front the cash required to do the shop?

Doing several reimbursement shops can mean putting purchases of hundreds of dollars on your credit cards, or laying out the cash. Do you have the cash or available credit to do this? And if you are not paid by the time your credit card bill is due, will you have the funds to pay the bill in full so you do not incur interest charges?

Choose your mystery shopper assignments wisely, to maximize the return on your time and effort. That may include doing at least some reimbursement-only shops, when the circumstances are right for you.

Is Partial Reimbursement Good Enough?

Although most of the time the reimbursement offered will cover any required purchases, there are some shops that offer a reimbursement that subsidizes the cost of the mystery shopper's required purchase but doesn't cover it in full. That means that you are paying money out of your pocket—money you will not be reimbursed—in order to complete the shop.

Are there ever times when you would find such a shop worthwhile? Perhaps, but you should be aware of the choice you are making when you select such an assignment.

Let me give you an example. I was looking at a fine dining shop that requires purchasing the following:

2 Beverages in the bar

1 Appetizer

2 Entrees

1 Dessert

2 Beverages

Looking at the restaurant's online menu, typical costs of these items might be:

$13 – $20 2 Beverages in the bar

$12 – $15 1 Appetizer

$40 – $70 2 Entrees

$8 – $12 1 Dessert

$5 – $10 2 Beverages

Order on the low end for each item and your total (before tax and tip) would be about $80. Figure another $20 for tax and tip and a few dollars for the valet, and that brings your total to more than $100. The reimbursement? $90.

In effect, you are getting a $100 meal for a little over $10, plus your labor. Is that a good deal? Maybe, if you can actually get out of there for $100 or so. That means ordering pretty carefully and choosing the lower priced items in each category.

The numbers in the second column above are not the highest-priced items on the menu, but ordering at that level takes your tab (with tax and tip) to more than $150.

Suddenly, your "free" meal is costing you more than $60 over your reimbursement.

In either case, you are getting $90 toward the cost of your meal, so let's look at this from another angle: What is your hourly compensation for this shop? If you assume about an hour and a half in the restaurant and a similar amount of time doing the report, that is three hours for $90, or about $30 an hour. Not bad, if you enjoy eating in nice restaurants and you view the reimbursement as payment toward something you want and value. Add travel time there and back, and the hourly rate drops a bit.

I will confess that I usually don't think of my travel time or the time I spend in the restaurant as work time. I am eating, and I have to do that anyway. We like to go out to dinner, usually at least once or twice a week, so I would be eating somewhere. It might as well be a mystery shop. (I know, I cannot be as relaxed on a shop as I can be when I am not working, but I have been doing this for a long time and it has gotten easier.)

If you mystery shop for cash to pay your bills, this is not a good shop for you. You are having to spend money out of pocket to do the shop, and you are getting reimbursed for something you might not buy normally. Because my husband and I enjoy eating out, and do so regularly, I might take a shop such as this. It would depend on how much I liked the restaurant.

I will say that over the last couple of years I have become less likely to take some of these shops. I love restaurant shops, but I resent it when the client treats my report as having the value of a coupon. Inadequate reimbursement is especially galling when I am forced to order more than I would have ordered in a normal situation.

The decision to take a shop that offers partial reimbursement is up to you, as you are the only one who can decide if it is worth your effort. However, you should know up front that the reimbursement is not likely to cover the entire cost of your required purchase. (I used the example of a fine dining shop, but this can happen with other types of shops, including casual dining and even retail.)

If you are not willing to do a shop for partial reimbursement, check out the client before you accept the shop. Determine what your required purchase may cost. Don't forget to add tax and tip to menu prices.

Mystery Shopper Pay via Gift Card – Good or Bad?

There are times when a mystery shopping company will send a gift card to be used on a mystery shopper job. Although rare, it's nice. You don't have to front the cash for any required purchase and wait for reimbursement. However, there is a trend in shopper pay that, in my opinion, is not quite so nice.

Some clients are choosing to reimburse mystery shoppers with gift cards, instead of cash. What this means is that you do the mystery shop and pay out of pocket for any required purchase. After your report has been accepted, you are paid with a gift card from the merchant.

Let's do the math to see if this is a good deal. Here is how it might work:

You go to a restaurant to do a mystery shop and pay $35 for your meal. Several weeks later, you get a $35 gift card in the mail. So you paid $35 and you got $35. All even, right? Well, not exactly. You have to go back to the restaurant to use the gift card. So now you have spent $70: $35 of your own money and the $35 gift card. Plus, you spent some amount of time preparing for the shop and doing the report.

In this circumstance, your mystery shopper pay is more like a "buy one, get one free" coupon than a true reimbursement. If they had reimbursed you in cash, you could take your $35 and go back to the restaurant again, or you could use the money to buy groceries, pay the light bill or whatever you wanted to do with it. Gift cards take away that choice.

But it could be even worse. Some reimbursement maximums are not sufficient to cover the reasonable cost of a meal for two people. In the example above, let's say that your bill (including tax and tip) was $45. You didn't splurge, that is just what it costs to eat there. A few weeks later, you get your gift card for $35, and return to the restaurant to use it. Again, you spend $45. Now you have spent $90 and been reimbursed $35.

There are times when I spend more than the maximum reimbursement amount on a restaurant shop. I know going in that it will happen, and we order as we always do (within the shop guidelines, of course). I view the reimbursement as my compensation for the time doing the report, and figure we would have spent the money on dinner somewhere anyway, so I am fine with the deal. However, I would not be so fine with it if my compensation required me to go back to the restaurant and spend money again.

Are there ever times when being reimbursed with a gift card is a good thing? Sure. It depends on how the reimbursement is structured and the shopper's preferences. For example, if there is a client you expect to shop on a regular basis, and you may use the gift cards to pay when you do future shops, your cash flow will be improved. Here is what I mean: You do the shop the first month and pay $35. The next month, you return and pay with the gift card you got for the first mystery shop. Repeat monthly. This may be worthwhile if you like having a monthly dinner at that restaurant.

Another possibility is when there is a standard reimbursement that is more than you would actually spend. In the restaurant example, let's say that you dine by yourself (if allowed by the guidelines) and spend $20, while still receiving a $35 gift card. You could then return to the restaurant with your spouse, or take someone out to celebrate, with your $35 card. Or you might give the gift card to someone instead of buying them a gift. If this is money you would have spent anyway, this could be a good deal.

Only you can decide if being reimbursed for your secret shopper purchases via gift card is a good deal or not.

You may find that, as in the above examples, you are willing to accept these mystery shopper jobs under some circumstances but not others.

Find what's hot, find what's just opened and then look for the worst review of the week.

There is so much to learn from watching a restaurant getting absolutely panned and having a bad experience. Go and see it for yourself.

Gordon Ramsay

CHAPTER 6

Preparing for the Shop

Before going to the restaurant you need to familiarize yourself with the shop requirements. Are there items you need to order? Items you shouldn't order? What observations are needed? What aspects of the shop do you need to time? Carefully read the shop guidelines to learn exactly what you should do on the shop visit.

Learn the Menu

Become familiar with the menu before your visit by going to the restaurant website. By reviewing the menu ahead of time you can prepare a knowledge question about the food (e.g., "Are there nuts in the pesto sauce? What type?") and plan what you are going to order. Remember that you and your guest should order different items.

A menu with prices can help you determine what to order and stay within budget. Online menus may or may not have prices, but many location-specific menus do. If the restaurant features online ordering, you may be able to find prices there.

Preparing Your Companion

Although you may be required to do some shops alone, most restaurant mystery shops allow, encourage or even require you to have someone with you. This is so you look like a typical diner, as most people have a companion when they are dining out.

If your companion is not an experienced mystery shopper, it is your responsibility to make sure that he or she knows what they need to do to help you get a complete and accurate evaluation—and they definitely need to know what not to do, so they do not affect the integrity of the shop.

Your companion's error could cause the shop report not to be accepted by the client. That means you would not be paid, and you might even be barred from future assignments.

Here is how to make sure anyone with you on a mystery shop knows exactly what to, and what not to do.

Start by choosing your companion wisely. If your best friend is prone to blurting things without thinking, she is probably not a good choice. She is likely to give away the fact that you are the mystery shopper. Someone who is not good at following directions, or who may resent being told what to do, is also not a good choice.

Your companion must be someone who is willing and able to follow directions, and who will be discreet. They must understand that they cannot talk about the mystery shop with anyone else: before, during or after the shop.

Train your companion on the shop requirements. On most restaurant shops your companion would need to know if there are things that must be ordered (or that should not be ordered), if there is an amount of time you must spend in the restaurant, any limits on alcohol consumption and other requirements. They also need to understand that the server is required to suggest certain things (such as appetizers, coffee, dessert, etc.) and they should not ask for those items before the server has had an opportunity to make a suggestion.

Because most shops require that you order different items, my husband and I usually plan our order before we get to the restaurant. If it is an unfamiliar place, we download the menu from the restaurant web site so we can study it ahead of time. That way we can focus on the observations and timings we need, and not trying to make up our minds about entrees.

The best thing is usually for your guest to allow you to take the lead. That means in asking or responding to questions, deciding when it is time to go, paying, etc. If they are not comfortable allowing you to do so, they should not accompany you on mystery shops.

Let them know how they can help. Can they help you out by getting names? Checking the other rest room? Looking for a manager? If there is something they can do to assist you with the shop, let them know what it is and how to do it.

Teach them about general mystery shopping procedures. It may seem silly to ask how late they are open on the weekend when you saw a large sign announcing the hours on the door. Or to ask about the sauce on the special when you know you are ordering something else. But these may be requirements of the shop. Advise your companion that they should not jump in with answers or comments or interrupt your conversations with staff, as you are doing your job.

Stress the importance of confidentiality. They are not to talk about mystery shopping, or discuss any aspect of the evaluation, while on the shop. That means they are also not to ask you questions in the middle of the shop about what they are allowed to buy or do.

And confidentiality extends to the next day at work, the family party or anywhere else. They should not talk about the specifics of the shop or the fact that you are a mystery shopper with anyone other than you.

All information is on a "need to know" basis. Do not offer more information about the client, the shop requirements or the report than your companion needs to know. They do not need to know every question that you will be answering or "how they did" on the shop. They definitely do not need to know how much you are being paid.

If you are allowed to take your children on shops, you may want to keep them completely in the dark. Small children have been known to let secrets slip, and the fact that Mommy is doing a mystery shop is a big, juicy secret.

Prepare your companion effectively to guarantee that your shop goes smoothly. My husband has accompanied me on mystery shops for more than 20 years, and we have never had a problem. That is because I go over all of the requirements with him just before the shop so he knows what is expected. If something unusual comes up, he lets me handle it. We are a well-oiled, mystery shopping machine!

Can You Take the Kids?

Do not assume that taking your children with you is okay. Some shops are for two adults, and children are not allowed. This is especially true for fine dining. Others may allow you to take your children, but if the shop offer or guidelines do not specifically say that you may take children on the shop, assume you may not.

Many clients do not want children disrupting the shop and affecting the service and timing. Your children may be incredibly well-behaved, but other people's are not. Even if your children are perfectly polite and charming, having them there will probably be a distraction for you and affect how well you do your job.

If you want to take your kids, ask the scheduler if you may. And understand if the answer is no.

We just don't make and
sell food.

We give you an eating
experience that you'll
never forget.

Anthony T. Hincks

CHAPTER 7

Typical Shop Requirements

In this chapter, we are going to talk about what you should expect when you do a restaurant mystery shop. There is nothing that is "always" done one way in mystery shopping. The information here is a general description of typical shop requirements and you should always read and follow the guidelines specific to the shop assignment.

Pre-Visit Telephone Call

Many restaurant mystery shops will require that you call the location to make a reservation or ask a question before your visit. Sometimes you will be given a specific question to ask, but usually you are just to ask a question of your choice, such as the hours they are open, directions to the location, if reservations are available, etc.

The report form may ask how many rings before the telephone was answered, if the person who answered used a full greeting (e.g., their name, restaurant name, location and a greeting such as "good afternoon"), if you were placed on hold (and for how long), if they were able to answer your question, etc.

There are also shops that consist only of a telephone call. These are rare, but they may involve calling to ask about holding an event at the restaurant or some other specialized scenario.

Most will require that you get the name of the person with whom you spoke. Listen when they answer the phone so you can catch the name. Often, they answer with a rehearsed greeting, such as, "Thank you for calling Fred's Bar and Grill at the Pier we're having a fantastic day this is Angela how may I help you?" I wrote it as one long sentence because that is how it comes out! You have to listen carefully to make sure they included everything they are supposed to say and to get the employee's name.

Bar Visit

You may be required to visit the bar before or after your meal. This is not typically required for lunch visits, but may be for dinner visits. Generally, when a bar visit is required you are to be seated at the bar, not at a table in the bar area. Consider that when the restaurant is especially busy, the bar may be crowded and there may not be seats available at the bar.

When to Do the Shop

The guidelines will tell you when the shop visit is to be completed. Most restaurant mystery shops will specify a meal period such as breakfast, brunch, lunch, dinner or late night, and will define what that means. For example, dinner might be 5: 30 p.m. – 8:30 p.m. You will also be given a day or range of days in which the shop is to be completed. For example, a shop offer might say that the shop is to be completed:

Between 3/1 and 3/12, Dinner (6:00 p.m. – 9:00 p.m.). Do not do the shop on Sunday.

When you apply for the shop, you may be asked when you would complete the assignment. If you say you will do it on 3/5, you will be expected to do the shop on that date. Do not change the date without getting approval from your scheduler. There may be several shops scheduled for different meal periods and the client wants a number of days between each visit. If you want to change from the 5th to the 7th, that may bump into another shopper's assignment.

Clients usually want us to visit at peak times. If you are there when there is no one else in the dining room, your experience will not be typical. I once did a shop during the Super Bowl and we were the only two customers. I overheard the employees saying that there had only been three other customers in the previous few hours. I had no idea that NO ONE would be out during the game. (Note: I asked the mystery shopping company if they wanted me to do a re-shop, but they accepted my report.

I learned my lesson, and I would never do another shop during the Super Bowl.)

Although they want you to visit when they are busy, that does not mean that they want you there at insanely busy times. Most guidelines will say not to visit on Valentine's Day, Mother's Day, Easter and other major holidays.

When the guidelines say that, for example, the dinner period is 6:00 p.m. – 9:00 p.m., that means that the majority of the visit should take place during that window. Do not start the visit before 6:00. You do not have to be out the door by 9:00, but you shouldn't plan on arriving at 8:50.

Ordering Food

The shop guidelines may specify certain foods that you must order. More commonly, you may choose what you want from the menu as long as you meet the minimum order requirements (e.g., an appetizer, two entrees and a dessert). Here is what you need to know about how to stay within the guidelines while ordering.

Restaurant Mystery Shops and Food Preferences

Each of us has at least one food that we simply refuse to eat, and there may be others that we do not care for or should not eat. This may be due to health reasons, religious prohibitions or just personal preference.

Most of the time this is not a problem on restaurant mystery shops. The guidelines may state that you must order an appetizer, entree and side, but not specify the exact menu items to be ordered. There are shops (usually fast food), though, that will specify exactly which foods to order. Even if you may choose any menu item you wish, there may be limitations on special requests, such as asking for sauce on the side or substituting items.

So what if someone has a long list of foods that they cannot or will not eat? Can they still do restaurant mystery shops? Sure! Here are a few tips anyone can follow to make sure their food preferences do not clash with the mystery shop requirements.

Read the guidelines. If the full guidelines are available before you accept the shop, review them to see what you must order. Even an email offering an assignment will generally describe ordering requirements.

Most of the time they do not require that you order specific items, but sometimes they do. If so, make sure it is something that you can and will eat.

Consider your companion. Restaurant mystery shops often allow or require that you have someone with you. Does your companion have dietary requirements or preferences to be considered? For example, because my husband does not like seafood I would not accept a secret shop at a seafood restaurant. Your companion may be willing to eat things you are not. If there is a requirement to order something you will not eat, perhaps your companion could order it.

Know the menu. Most restaurants post their menus online, so you can review them prior to accepting a restaurant mystery shop. Make sure that there are dishes both you and your companion will eat.

Be cautious with special orders and substitutions. In general, when you are secret shopping you should not special order items that are not on the menu. You may be able to request modifications or substitutions, but read the guidelines to be sure. For example, you might be able to ask for your burger to be served without grilled onions, or that they substitute mashed potatoes for french fries. Some shops, however, specify that you not ask for any changes to the standard item, so verify what you may order before doing the shop. Those special requests could affect the time it takes to prepare and serve the food or create other complications that would affect the integrity of the shop.

Do not order "to go" unless allowed by the guidelines. If you must order something you do not want to eat, do not assume that you can order it to go and take it home. You may, however, be able to take a few bites then ask for the dish to be wrapped up for you. It all depends on what the guidelines say, so read them carefully. When in doubt, ask your scheduler. Leaving your food untouched may cause the staff to be concerned that there is some thing wrong with the food. They may want to replace the food or they may even comp your meal.

And what about alcohol? There are restaurant mystery shops that require the shopper to visit the bar before or after the meal, or even to eat at the bar. The shop may require that at least one alcoholic beverage be ordered. If you do not drink, or do not wish to drink "on the job," your companion may be able to fulfill this requirement.

Shopping Under the Influence (SUI)

There are bar and restaurant shops where you may be encouraged or even required to order cocktails or wine, but drinking alcohol on a mystery shop can create problems if it is not handled properly.

Becoming inebriated can mean that you do not get all of the information you need for your report. And if you are drunk enough, you may behave completely inappropriately and not even realize it.

I had to do a fine dining mystery shop where my husband and I were required to order drinks in the bar, then a bottle of wine with dinner. That is a lot of alcohol, but with planning and thought, we kept our wits about us and did not become intoxicated.

Here are some things you need to remember when drinking while mystery shopping, and how to handle your liquor without getting out of hand.

Understand exactly what the shop requires you to order. Often, you will have a companion on these types of shops. It may be that only one of you is required to order alcohol. In that case, you might arrange for your companion to have a drink at the bar while you sip a soda. If you are required to order more than one round at the bar, you may be able to order an alcoholic beverage one time, and a soda the other.

When you must order alcohol, order something that will have the least effect on you. A wine spritzer, or a mixed drink with ice, is probably better than a martini.

Do not accept a shop requiring you to order alcohol if you are a teetotaler. You cannot leave your drink in front of you, untouched, and expect that no one will notice. The bartender or server will think that there is something wrong with your drink and will want to make it right for you. They may even take the drink off your tab, so your receipt will not show that you ordered a drink. In any case, it will draw attention and that is not something a secret shopper wants to do.

Put something in your stomach before you start to drink. Most people feel the effects of alcohol quicker on an empty stomach, so eat something first.

Alcohol can also have a greater effect when you take certain medications. Be aware of how your medications interact with alcohol.

Drink slowly. The alcohol gets into your system more slowly that way, and it gives the ice a chance to melt and water down your drink a bit. When you order a bottle of wine, the server will often refill your wine glass before it is empty, so drinking slowly means fewer refills and less mindless drinking.

You do not have to finish everything you order. You can sip your drink at the bar and leave some of it in the glass. When you are required to order a bottle of wine, you do not have to drink the entire bottle. Have a glass of wine, then stop. Depending on the laws in your state, you may be able to take home the partial bottle.

You are responsible for making observations and writing the report, so you need to keep your wits about you. However, it is important that your companion not over indulge either. Your companion drinking too much can be a distraction for you, and can jeopardize the shop. The last thing you need is your companion drunkenly telling the server, "You're doing a great job. You will be very happy when you see the mystery shop report."

Do not drive if you are at all impaired. Unfortunately, we are often not good at judging when we should not drive. You can use a rule of thumb about how much alcohol puts you over the legal limit, but even being under the legal limit does not mean that you are capable of driving safely. The safest choice is to have a designated driver, call a cab or take public transportation.

Don't Be a Big Spender on Mystery Shops

One of the things I love about mystery shopping is that many shops include a purchase allowance or reimbursement. That allows me to get something I would normally pay for in return for doing the shop.

Several years ago, I did a lot of grocery shops where I received a generous reimbursement when buying groceries. I used these shops to buy my usual groceries and to stock up on non-perishables such as soap and paper products, things I had to buy anyway.

Many mystery shoppers look at these perks and benefits of mystery shopping as getting things 'free.' They are not truly free because you earn them with the time you put in doing the shop and report, but they can be good compensation.

The danger is that feeling that you are getting something for nothing can lead you to overspend on mystery shops. When doing a fine dining shop, you may have an allowance of $150 or more. So if you end up going over that amount you may look at it as getting a $180 meal for $30. However, there are some reasons not to overspend on mystery shops.

The first reason is that if you are like most mystery shoppers you are doing this to make money. If you spend more than you earn on every shop you are not making money. Yes, it is nice to get a big discount on things you buy, but it is even better not to pay anything out of pocket. Keeping your spending in line means that you are not paying to do the mystery shop.

Another reason to avoid going over the reimbursement limit is that being a big spender may take you out of normal customer spending patterns. Many companies will warn against doing things such as ordering the most expensive item on the menu. You do not want to stand out or be memorable, so keep your purchases normal and reasonable.

Mystery shopping is not something for nothing, but it is a great way to get things you want or need in return for your time and effort.

Can a Mystery Shopper Take Home Leftovers?

I received this question from a mystery shopper:

I just got my first fine dining assignment, and I can't believe how much food we have to order! The instructions say that the mystery shop is for two adults, and we have to order an appetizer, two entrees, two side dishes and dessert. We usually share one meal, so I know we can't eat all of that! Can we order one of the meals to-go? Would it be okay if we brought home a doggie bag?

First of all, congratulations on getting the fine dining shop assignment. They can be a lot of work, but you usually get to enjoy a really good meal in a nice atmosphere. It beats the heck out of a lot of jobs I have had in my life!

As you should know, it is important that you follow all of the guidelines. That means that you need to order all of the required items, even if it is more food than you would normally order.

So can you get some of the food to-go, or take home the leftovers? Of course, the answers depend on the specific guidelines for your shop assignment, but here is how most restaurant mystery shops handle this.

In almost every dine-in restaurant shop you are to order all of the items to eat at the restaurant. That means no ordering to-go. If you are to place a to-go order, that will be clearly spelled out in the guidelines. To-go orders are not typical on dine-in restaurant shops, but you may see an assignment that requires it. Unless the guidelines specifically say to place an order to-go do not order any items to-go.

As for asking for a doggie bag, there may be shops that prohibit it, but every shop I can recall has allowed it. Even at fine dining restaurants. In fact, some have questions on the report form about how they handled the leftovers if you asked to take them home. (e.g., Did they wrap them up for you? Was there a note from the chef? Were they in a bag printed with the name of the restaurant?) That doesn't mean that you must take food home on those shops, but it clearly indicates that they expect you might.

When you know that you are likely to have leftovers, a little advance planning can help you make the most of it. My husband and I often have enough left over for our meal the next night. (Two nights where I don't have to cook? Yay!) Here are some tips on ordering and dining wisely:

Familiarize yourself with the menu. Most restaurants have online menus at their websites. Plan what you will order for the entire meal, keeping the shop budget and the tips below in mind. Some online menus do not include prices, but you can often find prices if you look for the location you will be visiting and pull up a menu specific to that location.

Think about what will transport and reheat well, and what may not be as good the next day. You probably don't want to take part of a salad home, for example. And the souffle? Not likely to work as a leftover. That may influence what you order, or it may determine which dishes you have just a bit of (and have wrapped to take home) and which you eat most or all of. The dessert with ice cream will be difficult to take with you, but cheesecake is pretty portable, for example.

Pace yourself. You need to eat some of everything. If you fill up on the appetizer, you will struggle to eat the rest of your meal. Eat a portion, then ask for the rest to be wrapped to take home. Most fine dining shops are not rushed, so give yourself some time to savor your meal.

Pace your alcohol consumption, too. Many mystery shops include a visit to the bar before or after your meal, and fine dining shops may require that you order wine or cocktails with your meal as well. Don't have a potent drink at the bar on an empty stomach if that is likely to make you feel sick (or drunk!).

If you order a bottle of wine with your meal, you may be able to take home what you do not drink. Check the laws in your state. Sip slowly and do not allow them to refill your glass unless you want more to drink. (Note: Some mystery shops do not allow you to order a bottle of wine, but I have done others that required it. As always, follow the guidelines for your assignment.)

Watch your language. Don't say that you didn't finish your entree because you are "saving room for dessert." That prompts them to offer dessert, and whether or not they do that (and how they do that) is probably among the questions to be answered on the report. The same goes for saying how full you are. If you say something such as, "I couldn't eat another bite," they may only offer coffee and not dessert. Or they may just bring the check.

My husband and I often use these tips to get a second meal from leftovers, whether or not we are mystery shopping. With restaurant portions (and prices) as large as they are, it is a good way to get value from your dining dollar or your labor as a mystery shopper.

What to Do With Food on Fast Food Shops

Question from a mystery shopper:

I do mystery shopping and get free fast food. I'm supposed to taste it but I don't want to eat the whole thing b/c I'm trying to stay healthy and I feel guilty if I throw it out and I also don't want to give it to anyone because I wouldn't even eat it myself. I'm CONFUSED!

Whew! First of all, take a breath. That second sentence is a long one! Although you are confused, there are several possible solutions to this dilemma.

Consider that your ideas about what you are willing to eat are not the same as those of other people. There is a reason that fast food restaurants sell as much as they do—lots of people like burgers and other fast food, even if you do not. If you know someone who would like the food, give it to them. They get to make choices about what they are willing to eat, just as you do.

When you give the food to others, they might have to be someone you know pretty well, because you will probably have to take a bite or two so you can report on the food. If you do not actually have to sample the food, you might give it to a homeless person or someone else who could use the meal.

The shop may have specific requirements about what you are to order, but if it doesn't, choose one of the healthier items on the menu. Most fast food restaurants have a wide variety of menu items, and some of them are better than others when it comes to fat, calories, etc. Or if there are parts of the meal you find objectionable (e.g., bread or French fries) don't eat those.

If you have to order something you do not want to eat and you don't have someone you can give the food to, throwing it away is better than eating something that you do not want. If you really think the food is as horrible as you imply, you should have no problem throwing it into the trash.

Lastly, have you considered not doing these shops? If you don't like the food and the idea of throwing it away is this stressful, maybe you should just say no to these mystery shops. Most of the time the reimbursement for food is a significant part of the compensation, so if you don't want the food they are probably not worth doing.

You do not have to accept a shop just because it is there. Do shops you enjoy that provide benefits you want.

How to Take Photos of Your Food on Restaurant Mystery Shops

More and more often, restaurant mystery shop assignments include a requirement that you photograph your food. It has often been a requirement in shops where the food was taken away from the restaurant location (e.g., take pictures of the pizza that was delivered) but now photos are often required for dine in shops, too. Even fine dining!

Although it might seem that taking pictures of everything would out you as the mystery shopper, it doesn't. Apparently we have reached a point in our civilization where we are so focused on Facebooking, Tweeting and Instagramming every moment of our lives, that taking photos of your food in an upscale restaurant is no longer considered odd. In fact, so many people post pictures of everything they eat to their blogs, Facebook, Instagram, Twitter and Pinterest, that you will probably not be the only person taking photos.

If you are not used to photographing your food, here are a few tips to help you get better quality photos and look like your standard-issue social media junkie and not a mystery shopper.

Read and follow the guidelines. The client will specify which items you are to photograph and what must appear in the photo. For example, they may want a picture of the entire plate taken from directly above. They may include sample photos in the guidelines. If so, review them so you understand what is expected.

When photographing food from above, watch out for shadows. Lighting in general can be a problem, especially in upscale, fine dining restaurants. (Yes, many of them now require you to submit photos with your report.) If necessary, use a flash.

Most smart phones can capture images that are far superior to the photos taken by quality digital cameras just a few years back. Using your phone should be fine, but read the guidelines to make sure your phone will do what is needed. There are also many high-quality point-and-shoot cameras that fit in a pocket or purse. You don't need a giant camera with a two-foot lens.

Remind your companion before the shop that the food is to be photographed. Typically, you have to take a photo of each item before it has been touched. If your partner digs in before you get the photo…oops. Your shop may be invalid.

Check your photos immediately to make sure you got what you need. Take additional photos, if necessary. Photos are a critical part of the shop, and if yours do not meet the requirements you may not be paid for the shop.

Take additional photos. Photograph your companion or ask your server to take a photo of the two of you together. If you are taking photos beyond the required food photos you may look like a lunatic, but you won't seem to be a mystery shopper. You are just capturing a special date night or fun evening out. (Be careful about saying you are celebrating a special occasion, such as a birthday or anniversary. They may comp a dessert or other item, and that could affect your shop. I have had some special occasion dinners as mystery shops, but I always cleared it with the mystery shopping company first.)

Although many people post photos of their meals to social media, do not post your mystery shopping photos there. Many clients do not want photos or comments from a mystery shop appearing online.

Act as though you have done this before. If you are uncomfortable taking photos or unsure of what you are doing, you will draw attention to yourself. Practice before your shop by taking photos at other restaurants. You might even start taking pictures every time you dine out, just to get in the habit and improve your skills. The great thing about digital pictures is that you can take all you want and it doesn't cost anything. (Remember film and getting photos developed? Ick.)

Photos give clients more information about what was served than a written description can, so taking photos of your food on restaurant mystery shops is a requirement that is likely here to stay. With a little practice, you can produce great photos with little effort.

If you want a reliable tip, drive into a town, go to the nearest appliance store and seek out the dishwasher repair man. He spends a lot of time in restaurant kitchens and usually has strong opin-ions about them

Bryan Miller

CHAPTER 9

Paying the Bill

In almost every case you will be required to pay for your meal at the time of the mystery shop, and get reimbursed sometime after your report is accepted.

Here are some tips about how to pay for your meals.

Cash or Credit Card?

Unless the guidelines say that you must pay with cash or you must use a credit card, you can pay however you wish. However, sometimes you will be asked to use a specific payment method. For example, you may be asked to pay with cash because the client wants to know how the cash was handled. Was the purchase rung up and the money put in the register immediately? Did they return your change or did they ask if you wanted your change back? Other times they may want you to pay with a credit card, or there may not be any requirement about the method of payment.

Tipping

When you mystery shop a restaurant where tipping is customary, it is typically expected that you will tip 15 – 20%. The tip is part of the allowable reimbursement, not in addition. If the guidelines say that you will be reimbursed up to $50, and your check total is $45, tipping about 18% ($8) will put you over the maximum reimbursement. That extra $3 comes out of your pocket. However, that is never an excuse not to properly tip your server. When accepting an assignment, and when deciding what to order, keep in mind that you are expected to tip and choose appropriately.

Valet

On some shops you may be expected to use valet parking service. Sometimes there is a charge for parking, sometimes not. If there is not a charge you should definitely tip the valet. If there is a charge to park, tipping the valet may still be appropriate. If you are not sure of the custom in your region, ask the scheduler what is expected and what will be reimbursed.

May I Use Gift Cards on Mystery Shopper Jobs?

A mystery shopper asks:

I got several gift cards as Christmas gifts, including some for stores and restaurants I sometimes visit as a secret shopper. May I use these gift cards on mystery shops, instead of paying with my own money? What about gift cards that are issued by the credit card companies (e.g., Visa, American Express), not the store or restaurant? May I use those on mystery shops?

Generally, you should be able to use gift cards on mystery shopping assignments. However, there are a few exceptions.

Some shop guidelines specify a method of payment. If the guidelines say that you must use a credit card, you must use a credit card and not a gift card. Gift cards, even the ones issued by credit card companies, are not the same as credit cards and should not be used when the client wants you to pay with a credit card.

I would also recommend not using a gift card when the guidelines specify that you should pay with cash. Even though gift card purchases are, in many ways, like cash purchases, they are not the same. For example, the client may want you to pay with cash because they want you to make observations about how the cash was handled. There may be questions on the report about whether the cashier counted back your change, if the cash drawer was closed immediately after the transaction, etc. If you pay with a gift card, you would not be able to answer these questions.

Most mystery shops do not specify that you use a particular payment method. In those cases, paying with a gift card would be fine. (Unless, of course, the guidelines say not to use a gift card.)

There are clients who now provide mystery shop reimbursements in the form of gift cards. If you receive a gift card instead of cash from the client, there should be no problem using the gift card on a future secret shopping visit.

May I Use a Coupon on a Mystery Shop?

In most cases, the client will not want you to use a coupon on a mystery shop. However, that is not true for all shops. If you have a coupon and want to use it, ask the scheduler if you may.

You may also want to consider if you really want to use a coupon on a mystery shop for which you are being reimbursed. Would you get a better value for the coupon if you used it at a time when you are paying the entire bill yourself, without any reimbursement?

CHAPTER 10

Completing the Report

After you are assigned a shop you will be given a report form to fill out online after the shop visit. Reports generally consist of a number of yes/no questions and areas where you are to write comments or narratives. Here are some tips on how to complete your reports.

Avoid Comparisons in Your Mystery Shop Reports

It would seem that a simple way to explain what something was like would be to compare it to something else. We do that all the time: "The movie was kind of like *When Harry Met Sally*, but not as funny."

However, unless specifically requested, you should avoid making comparisons in your mystery shop reports. Reports should include only information about what occurred during your visit, and should not reference any experience outside of that time and place.

Let's look at some examples of what you should NOT put in your reports.

"It took 17 minutes to get our food, but the restaurant was much busier than it usually is."

Just say that your entree arrived 17 minutes after you ordered.

"The parking is much easier at this restaurant than at the downtown location."

You might comment that you were able to get a parking spot right by the door, but do not compare it to another restaurant.

"I thought the prices were too high. The food is better at Jasmine's, and their prices are much lower."

This one is a two-fer: a comparison and an opinion. Neither of them belongs in your reports.

"Pat was much friendlier than the server who was here before."

That's just wrong. Say what Pat did, but do not compare him to anyone else.

"I like the menu selection better at LaRitzy Bistro."

By now you get the idea. No comparisons.

There are times when you are asked opinion questions that cause you to make comparisons. For example, you might be asked to compare this visit to a recent customer experience at another business. However, if you are not asked for comparisons, do not make them.

To sum up:

Do not compare one business to another:

"The portions are larger at Jack's BBQ."

Do not compare one location to another:

"The staff is friendlier at the mall location than here."

Do not compare one visit to another:

"Service here is usually prompt, but it was slow tonight."

Just give the facts as if this is the only time you have ever been to this location, and you have never been to any place even remotely like it, ever in your life.

Sticking to objective facts in your reports will always make them better and more valuable to the client.

Mystery Shopper Reports and Opinion Questions

Although most of the questions on secret shopping reports are objective, yes-or-no style questions, many reports include one or more questions that ask for your opinion. Examples include questions such as:

- Based on the service you received today, would you have opened an account at this bank?
- Based on the rental agent's presentation, would you have rented an apartment here?
- Would you return to this store/restaurant and spend your own money?

These questions call for your opinion, but a good answer requires that you back up your opinion with reasons and facts. Here are some examples of how to handle these types of questions.

First of all, read the question carefully. The question, "If you were looking for a bank, would you have opened an account with us today?" is not the same as, "Based on the service you received today, would you have opened an account at this bank?" The second question is all about the service you received from the bank employee, not about any of the products or services you were told about.

As for the basic yes or no answer, what does your gut say? If you were a "real" customer, would you have said yes to their offer or would you be willing to come back and spend your own money?

Does your yes or no answer jibe with the answers in your report? If the report is glowing, and they did everything right, but you say no, well, what is the problem exactly? Likewise, it will look odd if the report shows that you received terrible service and yet you want to do business with them.

Be ready with reasons to back up your answer, whether you answered yes or no. For example, perhaps the service was only so-so, but the food was delicious so you would return. Even if your report indicates everything was wonderful (or everything was awful) give one or more reasons why you would (or would not) select that business or return there.

Use an appropriate reason. When you mystery shop a business, you are pretending that it is a business in which you are interested. Answering that you would not do business with that bank because it is 20 miles from your home, or that you would not rent an apartment because you own your own home, is wrong. You must put yourself in the shoes of a potential customer who walked in the door because they would consider doing business there.

Another mistake is saying that you would not return and spend your own money because the prices are too high. For example, if you are evaluating a fine dining restaurant you should not say that you would not return and spend your own money because, "I would never spend $150 on a meal." You are playing the part of someone who would spend $150 on a meal, and the question should be answered from that mindset.

It might be appropriate, though, to say that the value does not compare to similar restaurants. For example, there is a well-known fine dining chain that, in my opinion, offers food and service that are not the same quality as others. If I were to mystery shop them and the report asked if I would return and spend my own money, I would probably say no, because there are other restaurants of that caliber that have more menu selections, better quality food, and more attentive service. The specific answer, of course, would depend on exactly what question they asked and how it was worded.

When you are faced with one of these opinion questions, the idea is to give an honest answer, backed up with facts as to why you answered that way.

Including Timings in Your Report

Most mystery shopper jobs require that you include several timings. These may include:

- The time you arrived and the time you left

- How long you were at the location before you were greeted by an employee
- The time between placing an order and receiving it
- How long it took to process your payment
- And many others.

Timings are vitally important to the client. Many of their standards to relate to client service times. Customers want speed and efficiency, and clients need to know that they are meeting customer expectations.

The client may ask for timings rounded to the nearest minute, or they may want them down to the second. How can you get the specific timings needed to make your mystery shopper reports accurate and complete? Here are some of my favorite tips.

Wear a digital watch. Trying to discreetly get timings from an analog watch can be difficult. Use a digital watch with a display large enough to read at a glance. Make sure the display includes seconds, as well as the hour and minute.

Get a stopwatch with a lap timer. There are many small stopwatches that attach to your keychain or easily fit in your pocket. Many digital watches also include stopwatches. You want a lap timer so you can capture multiple timings. The way it works is that you tap a button each time you want to capture a time. Learn how your stopwatch works and practice with it so you can get timings without looking at the stopwatch.

Use your cell phone. Your cell phone may include a stopwatch. If you can use it without drawing attention, that may be an easy way to get timings.

Make notes during the shop. Be very careful about making notes during a shop; however, if you are discreet, you can jot a few timings, names and other notes. Go to a closed restroom stall. Send yourself a text message. Jot a few notes on your shopping list or in your check register.

Back up your timings with a digital recorder. Record the shop so you can verify the timings you took during the shop visit. Do not rely solely on the recording—technology can fail. However, reviewing the recording can be a good way to double-check your timings.

Timings that do not add up will cause the editor to question your report. When you complete your report, check your timings against each other. For example, if you say you were at the location 32 minutes, but individual timings add up to 38 minutes, something is wrong.

Getting your timings right will make your reports valuable to mystery shopping companies and clients.

CHAPTER 11

Restaurant Mystery Shopping Tips

Mystery shopping a restaurant is more than getting paid to have dinner. Restaurant mystery shops require lots of details: names, timings, and much more. Do your preparation, follow the guidelines, and make good observations to do a great job on your shop report. Here are some tips for making your next restaurant shop easier and more successful.

The time of visit is important. You will be given a range of times, such as between 5:30 p.m. and 8:30 p.m. for a dinner shop. Don't do the shop outside of those hours.

You may be asked to get many timings during your shop. Fast food shops often require several timings to the second. Use a stopwatch with a lap timer to record multiple times. The stopwatch should be concealed in a pocket so you can time discreetly.

A digital recorder with a timer can be a good way to capture timings at fast food or full-service restaurants.

Restaurant shops often allow or require that you take someone with you. Your companion must understand any requirements.

Refer to the guidelines regarding how many people may accompany you. If the guidelines state two adults only, it means exactly that. Don't take more adults and don't take your children along. Having four people in your party but asking for two checks is not the same as having two people in your party. Don't even think about it.

If the shop includes a bar visit, pay attention to whether you are asked to visit the bar before or after dinner. Bar visits may allow you to order one or two alcoholic beverages per person. Typically, they may not require that both people order alcohol, but one of you will probably have to.

Don't be a big spender and order the most expensive items on the menu. Be a typical diner. That goes for tipping, too. The guidelines usually allow for a tip in the range of 15 – 20%.

Plan ahead. Go to the restaurant's web site and download the menu prior to your visit. You and your companion can plan what you will order. That way, during the shop you can focus on getting information and not studying the menu. You can also think of a question to ask about the food, if that is a requirement of the shop.

Don't make notes at the table, and NEVER bring out the report form or bring it up on your phone in the restaurant.

The report must be objective. The food isn't "poor" because you don't like anchovies.

Above all, as with any shop, be familiar with the shop guidelines so that you are able to meet all of the shop requirements.

Read the guidelines right away, and schedule the shop as soon as possible. Make sure you follow the guidelines for how many people may go on the shop, and whether children are allowed.

Make reservations before the day of the shop. Many shops require that you call ahead to verify hours of operation and make a reservation. Do not wait until the day of the shop to call. You may find out that they are not open on Mondays, or that there are no tables available. Call at least a few days ahead.

Do your research. You may be asked to come up with a question about the menu to ask your server. You will almost always be required to order different items. Go to the restaurant's web site and download a menu as part of your preparation for the shop. You can plan what each of you will order, and think up a question to ask. Also, if the menu includes prices, you can plan your budget.

Show up on time for your reservation. Being "fashionably" late may mean that your table is not available when you arrive. That may have a negative effect on the score the restaurant receives.

Do not make special requests regarding seating, unless it is specified in the guidelines. Turning down the table you were offered and requesting a booth may overload a server or create other problems.

Make sure your companion is properly trained for the shop. They should know what to order (or what not to order), how to behave on a mystery shop, how they can help you, and what not to do. Doing things such as ordering before the server can make a suggestion affects the integrity of the shop. As the pro, it is your responsibility to train any "civilians" who accompany you.

Get accurate timings with a digital voice recorder (DVR). A DVR can capture when you order, when items are served, when a satisfaction check is performed, when dishes are cleared, etc. Although you should still get timings in other ways (such as with a stopwatch or digital watch) the recording is a nice backup.

Be aware of laws regarding recording. Look them up here: https://www.mwl-law.com/wp-content/uploads/2018/02/RECORDING-CONVERSATIONS-CHART.pdf. If you are in a two-party consent state, you can still use the recorder. Just make sure you are not capturing the voices of others. Set it up so that yours is the only voice recorded, or use sounds (such as tapping the mic) to capture timings.

Keep your report comments as objective as possible. Food always brings out opinions and emotions, but they do not belong in your reports. The salad was not "poor" just because you do not like artichokes.

Give realistic answers to the competitive questions. Some reports ask things such as who you see as the primary competitors to this restaurant, or where you would have eaten today if you had not come to this restaurant. Answers to both questions should be based on the type of food and price category. Saying you would have eaten "at home" or a fast food restaurant is not the answer they want.

Four Things You Should Not Do on Restaurant Mystery Shops

There are some innocent mistakes that can affect the integrity of your shop, and maybe even get it rejected. Here are four things you need to avoid when you are mystery shopping a restaurant.

Do not ask for a particular table. The hostess may ask your seating preference (e.g., table or booth) and, assuming the guidelines do not say otherwise, you may tell her which you prefer. However, when she escorts you to a table you should not ask to be moved to another.

The reason? Patrons are assigned to tables so that servers are not overloaded. If one server gets two or three tables seated all at once, they are going to have a hard time taking care of everyone according to the restaurant's service standards and their performance will suffer. That is not fair to them.

Do not order "off menu." Ordering something they do not normally serve, or even asking for special preparation, complicates things and may affect the time it takes to prepare and serve your food. This can be especially important in fast food restaurants, where a few seconds can mean the difference between hitting a service standard or missing it. There are fast food shops that specify you may not order a burger without a bun, for example. In some cases you may ask for minor modifications ("Hold the onions, please.") but no major changes or substitutions.

Not only can asking for something out of the ordinary slow your service, it affects the product. I have done shops where I had to weigh the food or beverage I received. If you order your burrito with "no lettuce and no cheese" then it may not fall within the weight guidelines for that item. Read your guidelines carefully to know what you may and may not modify in your order.

Don't order the most expensive thing on the menu. Some shoppers think of a restaurant mystery shop as a chance to get "free" food and they order extravagantly. Order as you would if you were paying out of your own pocket. Stay away from the lobster and the two-pound porterhouse and order the sirloin.

An exception related to this is that restaurant mystery shops may require that you order more than you normally would. For example, you might have to share an appetizer AND dessert, as well as each ordering an entree and even a side. Always order the number and type of items specified in the guidelines, but you don't have to order the most expensive ones. You can order the chips and queso as your appetizer instead of the combo sampler platter, for example.

Don't let your companion "wing it." Restaurant shops usually allow or require you to have someone with you. It is your responsibility to make sure your companion does not blow the shop by giving away that you are the mystery shopper or not following the guidelines. For example, most of the time you and your companion will be required to order different entrees. Make sure she knows that. The report may ask if your server suggested coffee or dessert. If your companion asks to see the dessert menu before the server has a chance to offer it, he has affected the integrity of the shop.

Go over all of the shop requirements before the visit, as well as some mystery shopping basics, so your companion can be an asset and not a liability.

Following these four rules will help you to provide a report that accurately measures the service you received, and will make you a valued restaurant mystery shopper.

The Month of Free Food

My husband and I like to eat out in restaurants, and we usually do so at least once or twice a week. A while back I accepted several restaurant mystery shops we could do for our usual date night dinners, and my husband joked about it being "the month of free food." (Of course, it is not really free because I have to work for it. But I guess it is free to him!)

I only did one or two restaurant shops a week, but his comment got me thinking: What if I really tried to get "free" food every day for a month? How would I do it?

Let's play with this hypothetical for a bit, because I think you may get some ideas about how to get more of the shops you want, whether they are shops of restaurants or other businesses: stores, banks, apartments or whatever you like to do.

First, to get the best selection of shops you would want to be registered with as many legitimate mystery shopping companies as possible. The more shops you have access to, the greater your chances of filling in all of the gaps and getting the number of shops you want.

Start with my free list of mystery shopping companies at https://www.mysteryshoppersmanual.com/mystery-shopping-companies.

You will need to plan ahead to get the best shops. Those usually go fast. Many companies start releasing shops for the next month no later than the 20th, so be ready to start claiming the shops you want and filling in your calendar.

Consider starting with the self-assign job boards. You will know right away what shops you have confirmed, then you can start filling in more days.

Talk to a few schedulers you work with regularly. Let them know you are looking for extra shops this month and see what shops they might be able to send your way.

Check job boards, such as Jobslinger.com to find more companies and jobs. Even if you have applied to many companies, you probably have not applied to every company. You may find new opportunities on job boards. Jobslinger aggregates available assignments from several legitimate boards, including the Mystery Shopping Providers Association.

When you see a shop you want, apply right away and make sure your application is complete. Many times they ask a question such as what day you will do the shop, or if you will do the shop by the deadline. Be sure to answer this question if you want to get the assignment.

Be open to a variety of shops. It might be nice to do one or two fine dining shops, but you wouldn't want to do those every night, even if you could. Mix it up with different types of food and restaurants, everything from fast food to pizza to casual dining to more deluxe choices.

Some restaurants have carry out shops where you phone in an order or order online, then go pick it up. I like those because they often have the same reimbursement as a dine in shop, but the reports are shorter. (Hey, we take our shortcuts wherever we get them!) Save a little time by looking for a few of those, as well as some drive-through shops.

You may also save some time by doing more than one shop of the same chain. You probably cannot visit the same location more than once in a month, but you may be able to do multiple locations. When the requirements are the same, it takes a little less effort to prepare and do the shops. (Never take shortcuts such as copying-and-pasting from one report to another and always review the guidelines to make sure the requirements are the same.)

So will you be able to schedule a restaurant shop for every day of the month? I would be open to a little "fudging" on this to hit the goal. For example, we often bring home leftovers when we dine out. That is especially true when we are doing a mystery shop and may have to order an appetizer and two entrees, then save room for dessert. If all I am doing is reheating leftovers for dinner, I think I can count that as another "free food" night.

I have also done fast food shops where I ended up with extra meals after ordering in-store and at the drive-through, so one or two of those they could also take care of a second day's main meal. And with a few grocery store shops you may be able to get enough "free food" for at least a few more meals.

Okay, you get the idea. Of course, you could also apply this to other types of shops. What if you broadened this a bit and set a goal to get something you need "free" every day? Or to make a certain amount in fees and reimbursements?

Be aggressive about going after shops and taking on assignments you normally wouldn't consider. Look for opportunities to set up routes and do a group of shops one after another, or pick up a shop or two on your way home from your "real" job. Your goal doesn't have to be per day, it can be per week or for the month overall.

Although there are some shoppers who go about looking for mystery shopper jobs with what Dave Ramsey would call "gazelle intensity," most of us pick up a few assignments here and there as we have time. Being gazelle intense for a month or so could be a good way to jumpstart a stalled mystery shopper career or (if you focused on fee-only shops) a way to get cash to pay off an unexpected bill or save up for a special vacation or family treat.

CHAPTER 12

How to Become a Mystery Shopper

Most businesses with secret shopping programs do not directly hire their own shoppers. They hire mystery shopping companies who run the programs and select shoppers. Many mystery shopping companies are members of the Mystery Shopping Providers Association.

The first step is to apply online to mystery shopping companies. Never pay a fee to apply to any mystery shopping company. Legitimate companies do not charge you to apply. There is a list of more than 150 legitimate mystery shopping companies at http://www.mysteryshoppersmanual.com/mystery-shopping-companies. Although you do not have to apply to all of the companies listed, applying to several (perhaps 10, 20 or more) will help you to find more mystery shops faster.

Although some companies specialize and only shop in certain industries (e.g., banking or apartment communities) you will see that most mystery shopping companies work across a broad variety of industries. Even if your primary interest is in mystery shopping restaurants, be open to other opportunities and you may discover that you enjoy many types of shops in addition to restaurants.

Do not limit yourself only to companies located in your city, state or province. Many mystery shopping companies are national or even international. They need shoppers everywhere they have clients. I live in the Houston, Texas area, and I have mystery shopped for companies located in Texas, California, Florida, Wisconsin, Washington, Massachusetts and many other states. Although the mystery shopping companies were located all over the country, all of the shops I did for them were within several miles of my home.

Take time with your applications. Answer every question. Mystery shopping companies value shoppers with good spelling and grammar skills, so proof your application carefully before submitting it.

Mystery shopping applications ask a lot of questions. Their clients may have specific requirements and they need to find shoppers who meet those requirements. They may want shoppers who are within a specific age range, or who have a certain level of household income. Although most restaurant shops do not have a lot of specific requirements, many other types of shops do. The more information you provide on the application, the greater the number of shops for which you may be considered.

Answer every question on the application. When they ask for a writing sample, provide a short description of a recent customer service experience. They want to know that you possess good writing skills and also that you can write a detailed but objective narrative describing your experience.

Most applications will ask for your Social Security Number. That is because if they pay you more than $600 in a year the mystery shopping company is required to send a 1099 form to you and to the IRS. Some companies will allow you to hold off providing the SSN until you get close to $600 in fees, but many want you to provide it before you will be considered for any assignments.

Giving your SSN to a mystery shopping company is no more dangerous than giving it to anyone else. It is never 100% safe, but the companies secure their data and make every attempt to keep it out of the wrong hands. Of course, we read every day about data breaches at companies large and small, so we know that nothing is completely secure.

There is an alternative to providing your SSN, though. You can get a free Employer Identification Number (EIN) from the IRS and use that instead of your SSN. Although it is called an Employer Identification Number, you do not need to be an Employer to get one. Many Independent Contractors use EINs instead of giving their SSNs to every company with which they work. Just go to https://www.irs.gov/businesses/small-businesses-self-employed/how-to-apply-for-an-ein, fill out the form and in just minutes you will have an EIN.

The EIN can be used instead of a SSN when working as an Independent Contractor, but it cannot be used in place of the SSN in other situations, such as applying for a credit card.

Avoiding the Scams

You have probably heard about mystery shopping scams. In fact, some people think that all mystery shopping offers are scams. That is not true, as you have learned in this book. However, there are scams out there. Fortunately, there are three simple rules that will keep you scam-free.

Never pay to apply for mystery shopper jobs.

Never sign up for "trials" or "offers," especially anything requiring a credit card.

Never, ever cash a check and wire money (or send the PINs from pre-paid cards) to anyone for any reason. That is always a scam.

For More Information

Your first mystery shops will probably not be glamorous and you will not get rich. However, if you do a great job on those first shops, you will see more and better assignments.

My book, *The Mystery Shopper's Manual,* provides lots of great advice and tips for becoming a successful professional shopper. It is available at Amazon.com and my website, https://MysteryShoppersManual.com/.

I also offer a free online course on mystery shopping, and lots of tips and resources at https://MysteryShoppersManual.com.

If you receive a check in the mail saying that you have been selected as a mystery shopper, and asking you to wire money to someone, DO NOT CASH THE CHECK. See this article from the Federal Trade Commission about the mystery shopper scam.

http://www.ftc.gov/bcp/edu/pubs/consumer/credit/cre40.shtm

Look at your waiter's face. He knows.

It's another reason to be polite to your waiter: he could save your life with a raised eyebrow or a sigh.

Anthony Bourdain

CHAPTER 13

What's Next?

Now you know what you need to do to get started as a mystery shopper and get paid to evaluate your favorite restaurants. The rest is up to you!

Let me know about your experiences as a mystery shopper. My personal email address is cathy@idealady.com. Let me know about your successes, or how I can help you overcome an obstacle.

Here's to your success!

Cathy Stucker
https://IdeaLady.com/

A great restaurant
doesn't distinguish itself
by how few mistakes it
makes but by how well
they handle those
mistakes.

Danny Meyer

About Cathy Stucker

Cathy Stucker is The Idea Lady. She helps entrepreneurs, professionals, authors and publishers build expert reputations and attract customers with techniques that make marketing easy, inexpensive and fun.

Cathy provides hands-on help through her consulting services, and teaches clients as well as do-it-yourselfers in seminars and teleclasses. She also publishes manuals, special reports, booklets, audio and video programs and ebooks with step-by-step instructions anyone can use successfully.

Cathy Stucker has instructed courses for a number of colleges and universities, and has presented seminars for many continuing education programs, community and business organizations.

Cathy is a frequent media guest. In addition to many appearances on Houston-area television programs, she has appeared on radio programs from coast to coast. Cathy has been featured in stories in *The Houston Chronicle*, *The New York Times*, *Woman's Day*, the *Associated Press*, *Woman's World*, *Black Enterprise*, and many others.

When she is not being written about, Cathy is writing. And she is a prolific author and publisher. Her articles have been published in national magazines and other print and electronic publications. She has created a variety of information products to educate entrepreneurs and others, and one of her publications is in the collection of the George H. W. Bush Presidential Library.

How Can You Contact Cathy?

For more information about Cathy Stucker, her products and services, visit her web site at http://www.IdeaLady.com. To request a free subscription to her newsletter, IdeaLady Insider, visit http://www.IdeaLady.com/. For more information about her products and services, or to schedule an interview, call her at 281-265-7342. Cathy can be reached via email at cathy@idealady.com.

You can learn more about Cathy at http://ConnectWithCathy.com/.

www.ingramcontent.com/pod-product-compliance
Lightning Source LLC
Chambersburg PA
CBHW061039050726
47592CB00004B/1512